LEADING *with*

Aliveness

Opening to the Deepest
Powers of Leadership

METTE NORGAARD

NORDIC PRESS

First edition 2025

Cover and book design by Sheila Parr
Author photo by Dani Vázquez

The Aliveness Effect model art by Liya James
The Aliveness Effect model © Mette Norgaard

Image of *The Great Wave off Kanagawa*
by Hokusai used under license from
Shutterstock: 2591349611 / Rawpixel.com

Paperback: 979-8-9997783-0-7
Ebook: 979-8-9997783-1-4

Published by Nordic Press
www.mettenorgaard.com

Contents

Opening

THE QUEST

LEADERS ARE GETTING HIT FROM all sides: cascading crises, geopolitical instability, runaway technologies, and the erosion of human connection. We are in a relentless state of readiness, bracing for the next blow. But when we are reactive, we cannot lead.

Leadership is movement; it is bringing people from where we are today to where we want to be tomorrow. Thus, we cannot meet the moment by retreating or armoring up. We do it by showing up, fully present, fully alive—what I call *leading with aliveness.*

For decades, I have been a student of leadership. I have worked with hundreds of leaders as they dealt with the aftermath of 9/11, the financial crisis, hurricanes, and the pandemic. In a world that is coming apart, I have stayed close to what holds us together—to what makes us more human, more potent, more whole.

To that end, this book is based on enduring principles and embodied practice.

The human species has faced periods of extreme destabilization and destruction before,[1] but this time, it is not only nations, continents, or empires that are at risk; it is the vitality of our planet. To meet the moment, we must remember who we are and where we come from.

OUR HIDDEN WHOLENESS

The *primordial force*—the creative fire that brought forth galaxies, stars, and the Earth—pulses within us. The *life force*—our biological lineage—passed from the sun to the plants, insects, and mammals—belongs to all living beings. But we forget. So we hunch, tap, stoop, and stress. Leading with aliveness is being present to this infinite source of energy in ourselves and seeing it in others.

The Great Wave off Kanagawa by Hokusai captures that primordial power: pure, undiluted potency. It signifies the turbulence that lies before us and the strength that lies within us.

I grew up by the North Sea, and the fierceness of those waters shaped my ancestors as it shaped me. It was a poor region, yet we were a proud people because we belonged to something vast and untamed. In the words of the old Danish song, "I am a child of the ocean blue realm." To this day, when the sea is in a stir, I turn my face into the wind, fill my chest with salted air, and open to the wild beauty of the world.

When we remember that we belong to something vast, we can face the magnitude of what lies before us. As leaders, we can see the satellite images of the storm and show up where it matters. We can find the strength to step into the boat and the skill to bring us home.

To comprehend such forces, we humans rely on ancient symbols. The polarities of yin and yang, up and down, day and night are profound. They show the way that opposites are complementary and reveal the hidden wholeness.

This duality has been rendered in many ways. I am drawn to the yin-yang of *movement and stillness,*

acceleration and slowing down, for it speaks to these times. The faster things move on the periphery, the more the center condenses—slowing, gathering, becoming still. In this stillness lies strength, the capacity to act.

On the surface, we advance with strategy, strength, and stretch. At the core, we open to spaciousness, stillness, surrender. We construct our identities on the periphery and then return to stillness, to source. The further we reach, the deeper the return.

Leading with aliveness is *not* about indulging our emotion or amplifying the drama; that's opera. And while the music is rousing, as in Verdi's *La forza del destino*, everyone dies in the end.[2] Leading with aliveness *is* about slowing down so we may heed the better angels of our nature and exercise ever-better judgment. It is moving with clarity, coherence, and commitment—full-bodied intention.

SOURCES OF STRENGTH

To lead with aliveness, we open to the universal energy—feeling its force, finding its form, and shaping it through practice. Inspired by martial arts, this practice takes form through the Power of the Pause: our capacity to stand in the eye of the storm. From there, the other powers unfurl like sails in the wind, and, when we catch that wind, we lead with perspective, practice, the pride, and play. The effect is expansive—I call it *the Aliveness Effect*.

The Power of the Pause is simply being, sensing the beat of the heart and the pulse of the universe. *With the pause*, we open to something vast—call it nature, the divine, or the cosmos. *Without the pause*, we get off center, scramble the signal, and amplify the noise. We miss our cues; the timing is off.

The Power of Perspective is deep attention, seeing the world as it is, not as we wish it to be. *With perspective*, we absorb information, discern patterns, and point the way. We go in straight and keep it simple. *Without perspective*, we confuse urgency with importance; we mistake activity for achievement—always busy, never bold.

The Power of Practice is embodied intention: the integrity of being. Pure presence. *With practice*, we gain confidence; from confidence comes relaxation

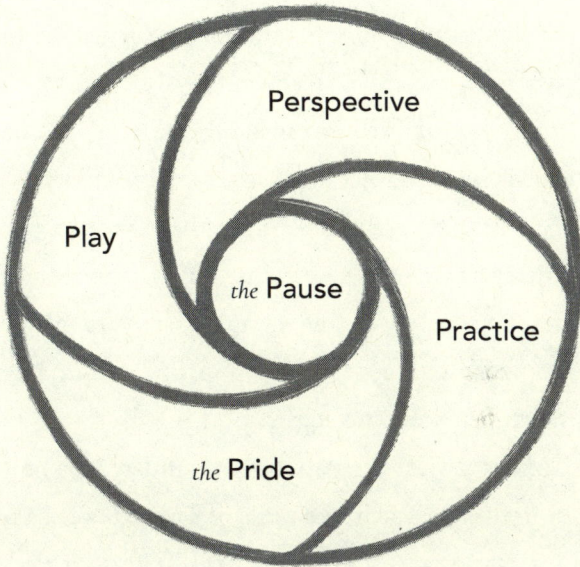

The Aliveness Effect

and flow, then timing and speed. *Without practice*, we lack inner strength and stability. In Chinese, such a person is said to have an "empty frame," to be "easy to push."

The Power of the Pride is optimal performance. Like a pride of lions, it is a collective presence, a coherent force. *With the pride*, each person is fully who they are and fully part of the whole. *Without the pride*, we live the tension: "Am I for myself or for the whole?" We second-guess every decision.

The Power of Play is pure adventure, at the edge of what is known, in contact with the unknown. *With play*, we are absorbed, drawn by the puzzle of paradox and intrigued by uncertainty. We surrender to the moment; we open to the ecstatic. *Without play*, we are left with choreographed spontaneity and staged creativity—no breakthroughs.

We begin with the pause, open and receptive, the portal to flow. We soar like the hawk entering the thermal updraft, wings wide, body still. It doesn't flap; it yields. And in yielding, it rises.

With the powers of the pause, perspective, and practice, we pay attention to ourselves and our capacity to lead. With the powers of the pride and play, we direct the attention of others so they can connect and create. We create cultures of vitality—that's the aliveness effect."

THE QUESTION

As we explore what it means to lead with aliveness, we will move from wilderness solitude to the top of a skyscraper, from the prides on the savanna to the crews in space, and we will do so in five easy chapters. First comes the story; then, we explore the power.

Leading with aliveness is not about stages or steps explaining the *how-to*; it is an invitation *in-to* your inner life as a leader. Along the way, we will look at leadership through fresh eyes, using fresh language, as we replace management jargon with ordinary words. We will think for ourselves. And we will answer a vital question: What power do we actually have?

———

THE POWER OF THE

Pause

WHAT STOPS YOU?

LEADING WITH ALIVENESS IS RECOGNIZING that each moment carries both risk and revelation—and stepping forward anyway. While writing this book, I co-led a retreat with fifty directors and board members who moved in such way. Their work was in the poorest and most violent cities in the United States, where they were giving children a path to, and through, college.

The second day of the retreat, I found myself next to Jim, one of the directors, as we watched the sun rise, and afterward, I got to hear his story. It began when Jim, as a volunteer, returned from a camping trip with a group of students from the UrbanPromise Academy. Bruce, the founder of UrbanPromise,[3] was there to greet them.

"How did it go?" Bruce asked.

Without thinking, Jim said, "You know, if I could

really do what I want to do in life, it would be to figure out a way to do this full-time."

Bruce looked at him. "What stops you?" he asked quietly.

Jim remembered thinking that was a stupid question. As a fifty-three-year-old business owner from a prosperous community fifteen miles down the road, he thought it was obvious what stopped him.

Still, the question kept gnawing at him. Two weeks later, Jim decided to put it to rest by telling his wife, Rae Ann, what Bruce had asked him. He was sure she would give him a list of what stopped him. But she didn't.

"Jim," she said, softly, "it's what you've been prepared for."

This is the voice of aliveness.

Within a year, Jim had sold the business, founded UrbanTrekkers, and begun a new adventure as "Mr. C"—one that would open teenagers from Camden, New Jersey, to the wonders of the natural world.

UrbanTrekkers began with outings to local mountains and rivers, where the students learned to hike, climb, camp, swim, and canoe. By the last year of high school, they were ready for the ultimate adventure: the Senior Rite of Passage.

The first cohort began with a grueling twenty-mile loop over the summit of Mount Marcy, New York. Next, they looked up at seventy feet of sheer vertical rock, facing their first climb. Finally came the ultimate adventure: the overnight, solo experience that carried both risk and revelation. As they stepped into the boat that would take them each to their separate islands, they grew quiet.

During their time alone, they were to see themselves at fifty years of age and, from this vantage point, write a letter to their current selves—a letter with the life mission they wanted to hold and with guidelines for the life they intended to live. Then, they were to find a symbol of something they needed to release in order to move forward.

Most would be leaving Camden for college, and Jim kept tabs on all of them. He recounted a conversation with one student, Terrón, before his graduation with a degree in accounting. Terrón had been apprehensive about college because "when you tell someone you're from Camden, all they see is the five o'clock news."

He paused, then continued in a raw voice, "But I had another story. UrbanTrekkers gave me my stories! When I had papers to write or was just chillin' in the dorm, I had my own stories."

Such stories are stored in our bodies; they are a shortcut to the Power of the Pause—a state of simply being. All it takes is a photo or a journal note to bring us back.

FINDING THE PAUSE

The Power of the Pause is being attuned to the body and open to the universal—be it nature, humanity, the cosmos, or the divine. It is embodied and transcendent. Timeless.

The pause opens us to the existential questions: What have I been prepared for? What brings me alive? What stops me? In time, as we sense our essence, anything nonessential simply falls away.

Today, the persistent uncertainty and the chronic "not knowing" keep us on the edge. They disrupt sleep, impair memory, and scramble internal cues on when to move, pause, or pivot.[4] We are unsettled, the opposite of what people need.

Thus, it is vital to pause and to remember we belong to something vast—that "we are made up of the same atoms and the same light signals as are exchanged between pine trees in the mountains and stars in the galaxies,"[5] in the words of physicist Carlo Rovelli.

We tap into the universal in moments of awe and express it in chills, tears, and *whoas*. Dacher Keltner, professor of psychology, has studied this phenomenon for more than twenty years, and these expressions are universal. In all cultures, we are moved by the wonder of the natural world and the moral beauty of others. By making music and mourning together. By a newborn's first cry and the dying's last breath.

We sense the spirit, and here I use the word in its original sense. In Latin, *spiritus* simply means the breath, animating principle, or life force—the very essence of the Aliveness Effect.

The Power of the Pause is simply being, whether we're wrestling with a life-changing question, just chillin' at the end of the day, or attending an executive retreat at Sundance.

THE SUNDANCE PROMISE

Sundance is a casual resort nestled in the lower ranges of the Rocky Mountains, and it was here that the Covey Leadership Center hosted Principle-Centered Leadership Week in the 1990s.

At the time, the book *The 7 Habits of Highly Effective People* by Stephen R. Covey was a global phenomenon. Leaders came from all over the world, the private and public sectors, and all branches of the military to reflect on life and the nature of leadership.

We began with the Sundance Promise: "If you will open yourself to the natural environment, the people around you, and timeless principles, you will find personal and specific answers to the leadership challenges and opportunities you face."

During the week, we explored the principles of leadership as we hiked up to Stewart Falls, read wisdom literature, and reflected on where we came from and where we were going. The Aspen grove became a metaphor for living systems and resilient cultures. The capstone would be a few enduring principles we could draw on as a source of security, guidance, wisdom, and power—principles we could turn to when riding high on success and when things came crashing down.

Stephen was in high demand, meeting with CEOs and heads of state, yet he was never rushed. Even when he returned from two days at Camp David, he just drove up the canyon and strolled in, ready for the Q&A. Stephen was known to say, "It's easy to say no when there is a deeper yes burning inside"—and he lived it.

IN STILLNESS LIES STRENGTH

Some leaders returned to Sundance every few years, and Doug Conant was one of them. By the time of FranklinCovey's[6] 2001 CEO Summit, he was CEO of Campbell's and I was preparing to lead the experience. Tied to the launch of Jim Collins' *Good to Great: Why Some Companies Make the Leap . . . And Others Don't*, the summit would feature Stephen and Jim and welcome twenty CEOs.

Then came 9/11.

Because I lived in New York City, the tragedy hit close to home. And when I flew out to Salt Lake City, the flight was eerily empty. It was an unnerving time.

I began the session by asking the CEOs if they had been personally affected by the attacks. One by one, they spoke of their financial partners who had died in the towers. Their spirits laid bare, they reflected on their losses and responsibilities. And I remember thinking, *Take off your shoes; you're on sacred ground.*

After a break, Jim shared his research on the *Good to Great* CEOs and their way of being. These executives embodied a powerful paradox: deep personal humility paired with strong professional will. And their humility didn't dilute their power; it concentrated it.

Sundance and the Executive Summit became the foundation for Doug's and my collaboration, first at the Campbell's CEO Institute and later at the Higher Ambition Leadership Institute.[7] Along the way, we walked, we talked, and we wrote the *New York Times* bestseller *TouchPoints: Creating Powerful Leadership Connections in Even the Smallest of Moments*[8] (in hindsight, the how-to for leading with aliveness).

Doug lived the Power of the Pause. He began every day taking his coffee outside as he watched the sun rise and the garden come to life. This was his time to reflect on the issues of the day, both personal and professional, and to "seek the right frame of mind to constructively deal with them . . . and sometimes say a little prayer." His intentions clear, he was ready for the day.

At his CEO Institute, we worked with twenty-four leaders at a time. The intention was to help them find their leadership voice so they could help others find theirs. Doug co-led every session. The inner resonance he brought into the room invited others to come alive in their own way and to realize how powerful they could be—together.

The first cohort began at the New York Stock Exchange, where we visited the Campbell's trading post and met with the chair of the Exchange. Two years later, we completed the journey in the Pocono Mountains, where the poet David Whyte took us beyond the ticker tape of time and into the transcendent. We then sat in silence, watching the bonfire, journals in hand—contemplating the life we intended to lead and our guiding principles.

We would soon need those principles as a source of security, guidance, wisdom, and power. A year later, Lehman Brothers went belly up, triggering the global financial crisis.

YOU WILL BE OPENED

Before going to Assisi, I spoke with a dear friend and Franciscan friar.

"You will be opened," he told me, almost like a prophecy.

"Opened to what?"

He smiled. "I don't know. To *sophia*, 'wisdom'?"

I went with a friend who knows Assisi well and who wrote about a book on the Power of the Pause in Danish.[9] We soon settled into the monastic rhythms of Lauds and Vespers, the physical rhythm of long walks in the mountains, and the hedonic rhythm of slow food and strong wines.

The fourth day was a holiday, and as the streets filled with tourists, pilgrims, and politicians, we escaped to Eremo delle Carceri. It was here, in this quiet oak forest with natural caves, that Francis and his brothers would seek solitude.

When I entered the cave of St. Francis, I was struck by the silence and sat down. There, walled in stillness, my breath deepened, my mind grew quiet, and time disappeared. My body began to rock as if moved by "big soft buffetings" that "would catch the heart off guard and blow it open" like the wind and wild ocean in Seamus Heaney's "Postscript."[10] Open to what? To the life force.

On future visits, spaced years apart, that opening would happen again. This energy is available to all of us when we are open and receptive.

———

What Power Do I Actually Have?

THE POWER OF THE PAUSE is rooted in a German proverb: *In der Ruhe liegt die Kraft*—"in stillness lies strength." The deep resonance of *der Ruhe, spoken in German,* deepens the breath and settles the mind. The harsh consonants of *die Kraft* are forceful and potent, as in the life force, *Lebenskraft,* or the primordial force, *Urkraft.* In inner peace lies power.

We have the power to

~ Give the body a sense of safety through daily routines.

~ Honor the body's natural rhythms.[11]

~ Create a space of inspiration we can tap into at any time (such as photos, music, quotes, journal notes).

Not knowing keeps us on edge. Stress hormones flood the system. Judgment falters. Burnout looms. The way back begins with physiological intelligence—knowing when to step back from the brink, when to give the body a break.

THE POWER OF
Perspective

COMPLEXITY AND COHERENCE

AS I WALKED ACROSS CAMPUS with Stacie, a neuroscientist and vice provost, we talked about what happens when you become a leader of leaders of leaders. The complexity is immense, and I suggested that the prefrontal cortex may actually change over time. She agreed and smiled, adding, "But that doesn't mean we're right."

Stacie had a light way of saying things, but she was serious about her work as head of research at a top university. At the time, she was six months into the role, with sixty-two direct reports and a scope expanding from research operations into research development and strategy. Stacie was studying the system—by listening.

"I am really interested in people," she said. "I want to know what they are thinking about their job, if they want to try new things, and how can I help." Stacie didn't summon her leaders to the top floor; she walked to theirs.

The shift from being a recognized expert to becoming a leader is often difficult, for it is also a shift in identity. But Stacie didn't hesitate; she was clearly a leader first and scientist second. She brought her whole self to the role.

I got to know Stacie during her year at the Higher Ambition Leadership Institute. Participating leaders referred to the experience as a gift of time because it gave them the space to step back and to gain perspective—on their leadership *and* their lives. A key takeaway was their personal model for how to lead people and change, one they would express as a metaphor, a formula, an acronym, or a story.

Stacie's model was profoundly human and based on interconnectedness. And, as a molecular biologist by training, she used the metaphor of a living organism: the brain.

She explained it this way:

The brain is a wonder of complexity and coherence. It is composed of neurons, and there are billions of neurons in the brain. And these neurons must connect to each other. You can't be sitting there alone; you have to reach out and make connections to other neurons, and the other neurons must connect back.

That's what she was building: a system grounded in relationships.

The brain can also be a metaphor for the enterprise, Stacie told me:

The brain is a pretty sturdy beast. You can have a stroke and still speak again. You can have a traumatic brain injury and still walk again because the brain has a lot of compensatory mechanisms and redundancies, which can see us through tough times.

Stacie leads from the inside out—not just cognitively but physiologically. Her model isn't theoretical; it is cellular. It reflects how she listens, adapts, and builds strength. Coherence doesn't come from commands; it comes from the way information moves, people sync, and aliveness spreads across the system.

GAINING PERSPECTIVE

The Power of Perspective begins with the capacity to direct our attention—to be clear-eyed about the world around us and attuned to the currents of change—but we live in a culture that profits from scattering it. Thus, it gets hijacked by algorithms and urgencies, and attention spans today are at an all-time low and dropping.[12]

This is the most disturbing trend in leadership today. For when we cannot direct our attention, we cannot gain perspective and clarify our intentions, and without intentions, we cannot lead.

So what can we do? We can outsmart the algorithms by activating the *extended mind*. We can turn to time-tested theories for leading people and change. We can expand the Aliveness Effect.

"If you want to truly understand something, try to change it," said Kurt Lewin, a keen observer of human nature and the nature of change. As a founding figure of social psychology, he also popularized the phrase "There is nothing so practical as a good theory."

Because when we use good research to inform our perspectives, we are in good shape.

Daniel Kahneman, the sage of behavioral economics, agreed. He believed we all stand on the shoulders of Kurt Lewin, and captured the essence of Lewin's Force Field Analysis this way:

> If you want to achieve change in behavior, there is one good way to do it and one bad way to do it. The good way to do it is by diminishing the restraining forces, not by increasing the driving forces. That turns out to be profoundly non-intuitive. . . . Diminishing the restraining forces is a completely different kind of activity, because instead of asking, "How can I get him or her to do it?" it starts with a question of, "Why isn't she doing it already?" . . . Then you go one by one systematically, and you ask, "What can I do to make it easier for that person to move?"[13]

Thus, the beauty of the question, "What stops you?" One thing that stops us is the skull-bound perspective of the mind. In 1998, philosophers Andy Clark and David Chalmers challenged this view in their paper "The Extended Mind," saying that we outsource our memory and other cognitive functions to our calendars and computers—that is, we think outside the brain.

Since then, research in neurophysiology, neuroscience, and cognitive science has opened us to a whole a new world of learning and leadership. In *The Extended Mind: The Power of Thinking Outside the Brain*, science writer Annie Murphy Paul distills this research into a coherent framework:

We think with our bodies—sensations, movements, and gestures.

We think with our surroundings—natural spaces, built spaces, and spaces of ideas.

We think with our relationships—experts, peers, and groups.

This perspective is wired into the way we work: We rely on it to shape the rhythm of the business, so everyone knows who meets with whom, when, and in what spaces. We use it when we move the energy with quick huddles and go outside for one-to-ones. We do it when we take the team to the mountains, so we can be together, think together, and create together.

Energy follows attention. It organizes around what is most articulate, coherent, and intense, strengthening the Aliveness Effect. Asking, "What stops you?" is more compelling than urgencies, and activating the extended mind is more stimulating than dopamine. Thus, we guide people's attention—by what we listen for as leaders and how we organize the work.

OPENING SPACES

Fortune's Brainstorm Design 2022 event in Brooklyn brought together 170 design-minded leaders from across the world to share our perspectives on the postpandemic workplace and the future. Every conversation began with the question, "What do you design?" My answer: "I open spaces for life to stream through."

To illustrate, I'd point to Pixar's co-founder Ed Catmull, who did so with just two principles: Story is king, and trust the process.[14] In an interview at *Fortune*'s Brainstorm Tech in 2019, Catmull was asked how Pixar picked the right idea for a movie, and he said:

We never take ideas from the outside, because a movie is not an idea. It is literally tens of thousands of decisions and ideas.

So what do they do?

We pick a director, who is then asked to come up with three ideas. Because then, when they get stuck, they can rotate through the other ideas, until they are prepared to present all three. Before the pitch, the directors inevitably say they love all three ideas equally, that it doesn't matter which one we pick.

Catmull laughed, then continued:

Now they're lying through their teeth. Because when they make the presentation, it's clear that they favor one. And that's the one we pick.

This is the way to open spaces for life to stream through.

BUILT WITH INTEGRITY

Aliveness is not about defining ourselves; it is about expanding ourselves, and as I stood on the top of the first all-electric skyscraper in New York City, I was ecstatic. The view was breathtaking, the design spacious, and the performance extreme; the tower was completed on budget, ahead of schedule, and with a stellar safety record.

Behind this achievement are the three founders of an architect-led development company. When I met them, they were completing their pre-COVID project and breaking ground on this one—an entire block in Brooklyn that would contain two schools and two high-rises.

Together, they hit the three notes on aliveness:

First, do the people you work with bring you alive? Clearly!

Second, does the work itself bring you alive? Yes! They did one building at a time, and each was a legacy project.

Third, does the way you do the work bring you alive? Not the way it used to.

That final note became the topic of our retreat to the Hudson Valley.

Jared, the company's CEO, and I drove up together and talked about the meaning of life, the universe, and everything. After we had settled in, the three founders were asked to reflect on their fifteen years together and what was to come. They then shared their perspectives, the personal and professional, the highlights and lowlights. And we then made dinner together.

As we lingered over the wine, Jared's reflections turned into a heartfelt rant. He had stopped by the site they were completing and found a mess of scattered tools, half-empty food cartons, and trash. Why couldn't people take pride in their work?! That opened a space for a new conversation.

On the high-rise they were about to build, they would be working with a new construction company. Might this be a chance for a reset? What if they were to build a culture of mutual respect and shared accountability? We decided to sleep on it.

The next morning, we cleared the schedule and set up two flip charts. Four hours later, we had a diagnosis and the initial design to share with the extended leadership team. That afternoon, I was meeting with a friend and retired colonel from West Point and invited Jared to join us. She told us how the Army embedded clarity at every level, beginning with the Commander's Intent—the desired outcome of the military operation.

A few days later, Jared met with the CEO of the new construction management company and shared their frustrations and failures with previous partners. After that, Jared asked a big question: "Would you be willing to entertain a new way of working together?" Leader to leader, they quickly agreed on a shared intention: to finish on time and on budget and to enjoy the process.

To adopt a shared set of practices, the CEOs then brought their leadership teams to West Point. There, each leader was paired with their battle buddy, their counterpart from the other company. Their commitment was, "If you need something, call me. If you're falling down, I'm going to come pick you up." They also adopted red teaming for planning and after-action reviews at every milestone.

Together, they created a culture in which people

treated one another and the worksite with respect. There was no graffiti, no vandalism, and no garbage. And instead of feeling defeated at the end of the day, people walked taller. For they were part of building a first—the first all-electric skyscraper in the city.

And this began with just three leaders who opened to one another and to the Power of Perspective.

A NEW YORK STATE OF MIND

I came to New York City in 1991, at the peak of the murder rate, a time when we had three locks on our doors and crack vials on the doorsteps. But, over the next few years, policing was reimagined, Times Square was cleaned up, business was booming, tourists were back, and we became the safest large city in the United States.

Then came 9/11, the financial crisis, Hurricane Sandy, and COVID. Each time, we were the epicenter of an existential crisis. And each time, the subway kept running, the rhythm adjusted, and the jobs came back. Because we have the talent and the tenacity to make it work. That's our perspective.

A year after 9/11, we honored the victims and heroes with candlelight vigils and concerts, and I found myself on the Great Lawn in Central Park. The New York Philharmonic opened with the somber and spacious chords of Copland's *Lincoln Portrait*, a tribute to human dignity and democracy. Meryl Streep narrated Lincoln's words: "Fellow citizens, we cannot escape history. The fiery trial through which we pass will light us down, in honor or dishonor, to the latest generation."

Wynton Marsalis and the Jazz at Lincoln Center Orchestra then followed with a New Orleans–style jazz funeral, starting in sorrow and ending in strength. It lightened our spirits—not because the pain was gone, but because we'd made room for it.

As we neared the end of the evening, we heard a single melody, and across the Great Lawn, our voices swelled: "O beautiful for spacious skies, / For amber waves of grain . . ." Our voices rising and bodies swaying, a year of grief had been shared and shed. The evening was complete.

That's when Billy Joel walked out, sat down at the piano, and pounded the opening chords to "New

York State of Mind." The lawn went wild! This was our Piano Man, and this rendition (accompanied by Marsalis) was raw and real, just like we were.

For in New York, we keep it real. We knew we were still a target; we knew we would recover—and we did.

What Power Do I Actually Have?

REMEMBER THE CLASSIC MARSHMALLOW experiment? Four-year-olds sat alone in an empty room, at an empty desk, with just a marshmallow before them. Their task was to *not* eat it. If they could wait until the researcher returned (fifteen minutes), they would get one more. A third of them made it. Their secret? The *strategic allocation of attention.* Instead of fixating on the temptation, they turned their backs, played with their fingers, made funny faces, or made up songs. Those who could direct their attention skillfully doubled their return on marshmallows, and they went on to lead more intentional lives.

We have the power to

~ Ask, "What if?" and explore multiple perspectives.

~ Frame a view that is coherent and compelling.

~ Use metaphor to express our way of leading people and change.

The problem is ever-shorter attention spans. If you cannot pay attention, you cannot direct the attention of others—in short, you cannot lead. Energy follows attention, and it organizes around that which is most intense and coherent. So step back and gain perspective, clarify your intention, and point the way.

THE POWER OF
Practice

THE SIZE OF YOUR SPIRIT

WENDY WAS A TINY WOMAN with an outsize presence and my instructor on Leadership Embodiment. She could cross nine time zones and still show up light as a feather and sharp as a tack, and at the dojo, she could throw men half her age and twice her size. What was the source of her power? A seventh-degree black belt in martial arts, decades of mindfulness practice, and the strength of her intentions. She didn't waste energy; she moved in straight.

"Size matters," they say in the dojo. "Not the size of your biceps, but the size of your spirit"—meaning our capacity to open to the energy that flows through the universe and all living beings—the life force, the ki, qi, or chi. Thus, we begin every practice by centering, connecting the embodied and the transcendent.

At the start of a workshop at Genentech, Salesforce,

or NASA, Wendy would say, "We're not going to use the F-word here. We're not going to ask you to talk about your feelings. That's because Leadership Embodiment is not based on psychology but on martial arts, and in martial arts, there is a lot going on, and it's very fast. You get attacked over and over again, and you learn to stay relaxed at that fast pace and to adapt and be creative." Then, she would lead a series of aikido-inspired drills and debriefs, which can be found in her book with Janet Crawford, *Leadership Embodiment: How the Way We Sit and Stand Can Change the Way We Think and Speak.*

In 2015, I was troubled by two trends and looking for a way to help. One was the way leaders amplified stress by talking about how busy they were, as if that were a badge of honor. The other was that leaders, with the proliferation in MBAs, were becoming more top heavy. They were savvy on strategy and skilled at managing the message, but they struggled to connect. The words were there, but there was no voice.

As a former physical therapist, I resonated with Wendy's work. Embodied leadership was deeper than physical intelligence; it was physiological. In my thirty years in leadership—practicing it, teaching it, earning a PhD in human and organizational systems—this was like the final piece in the puzzle.

One Saturday morning, I was leading a workshop on Leadership Embodiment with a few friends, including the CFO of a *Fortune* 500 company, the vice provost from a top university, and the CEO of a global NGO. They were all profoundly purpose driven and under a lot of pressure. We were there to turn this pressure into practice.

We began by centering: "Inhale up; lengthen the spine toward the sky. Exhale down the front; think of something that makes you smile. Extend your personal space out into the room, filling all four corners. Allow your shoulders to soften. And ask yourself, 'What would it be like if there were just a little more ease in my body right now?'"

For four hours, we worked with different partners, and their role was to get us off center with a frown, a gesture, a push, or a word. Our job was to notice and return to center. As we did the drills, the room filled with *wows* and *whoas*, for it's a wonder how light we can be when we open to flow.

We concluded by thinking about an upcoming high-stakes event. The CEO reflected on her trip to Davos, where she would be attending a small gathering with some of the most powerful business and government leaders in the world.

On her way back from the Alps, she sent us an email: "At the outset, my imposter feeling was in the red zone. So I stepped aside, took that deep breath, and rejigged my mind. The centering totally changed the situation: I owned my space and place in the room and engaged with everybody. Then, as the host suddenly called on me to take the floor—without even a minute of prep—I recentered, activated the quality of grace, and gave a powerful, slightly humorous, two-minute presentation." Pure presence.

The voice is embodied. It begins with the breath. A full breath allows for relaxation, and with relaxation comes resonance; it reverberates with who we are and what we care deeply about. The breath is the gateway to presence.

UNDERSTANDING PRACTICE

The Power of Practice is embodied intention. When we calm the body, we calm the mind; when we move the body, we move the mind; when we open our arms, we open our heart; when we point, we direct attention.

In *The Body: A Guide for Occupants*, Bill Bryson writes that it takes seven billion billion billion atoms to make you, and "for the length of your existence, they will build and maintain all the countless systems and structures necessary to keep you humming, to . . . let you enjoy the rare and supremely agreeable condition known as life."[15] Let us treasure this condition, as long as it lasts, for it does have an expiration date.

But Bryson also reminds us that the body is the product of three billion years of evolutionary tweaks and changes, and there are some annoying anachronisms. Beyond our control are two distinct patterns: One is reactive, the other resourceful. One gets us into trouble; the other gets us out.

Anything can set us off: running late, a curt response, or a presentation being cut short. That's human, and there's nothing wrong with that. But it becomes a problem when we indulge our emotions, amplify the drama, and spread it around. What's also human is our capacity to return to center. From there, we can dial up the urgency or slow things down, seek more information or act decisively.

The more we practice centering, the faster we recover—and speed matters. Because when triggered, we leap up Argyris's Ladder of Inference[16], moving from simple observations to self-righteous indignation. Then others get defensive, and so it goes. Thankfully, we have a choice: notice instantly, center, and smile. That's physiological intelligence.

MOVING WITH CONFIDENCE

Embodied Leadership is about inner coherence, which is central to the Aliveness Effect. When the head, heart, and core are united, we are powerful; when split, we lose power. Here's how it works. When making a decision,

~ The head considers the data: "Is this the rational thing to do?"

~ The heart cares about vitality: "Is it the right thing to do?"

~ The core does a gut check: "Do we have the will to see it through?"

When all three are all in, we are internally coherent. We move with authority, we show grace under pressure, we have executive presence.

Officiating the building. After my second session with a global IT leadership team, one of the leaders, Kevin, sent me an email. In his other life, Kevin is an ice hockey official who has officiated games with NHL professionals in the Olympics. On-ice officials like Kevin must project confidence, from something as seemingly benign as the pregame handshake to a championship game in which all hell breaks loose during double overtime.

As Kevin said in his email, "Sometimes, speaking from the head is all that is required. A simple recitation of the rule without any kind of attached emotion is sufficient. Other times, we need to bring passion to our calls to show that our level of engagement in the game is equal to that of the players and coaches. At *all* times, we must communicate with confidence." Confidence lies at the core, the body's center of gravity, the source of stability.

It's one thing to manage the pace of the game and the heat between players, but what about the fans? In our next session, Kevin took us beyond the rink to the entire arena. Officials must have the capacity to contain the energy of *everyone*; they call it *officiating the building*.

I call it leading with aliveness: each gesture free from hesitation, each move decisive, each moment complete.

Grace under pressure. Now, to the girl in the arena, to whom playing was like flying, and to the woman who helps others find their wings. Sheila was there when I asked the board members of UrbanPromise International about the source of optimal performance: Does it lie in the person or in the dynamics of the team? She raised her hand and shared her story.

One year, Sheila didn't particularly like the other players on her junior high basketball team. They weren't friends or anything, but they played hard, and they played well. And they went on to an undefeated season. Then, her face lit up: "There's nothing like an undefeated season."

Later, Sheila told me the season wasn't special just because they won; it was also because they moved as one. "When I was open," she said, "the ball was there, and I had that feeling of flight when I elevated to layups and in how I came down. I loved the physicality of it. I loved running up and down the court, and when I was off the ground completely, it was like I was flying."

What about her coach? Her features softened. "I loved and adored her." Sheila said. "She wasn't sweet and nice; there was none of that. But she saw me. She'd look into my eyes and state things very clearly, and I knew what I needed to do to be my best. She just saw me."

Being seen by someone we respect is a gift, and we can never pay it back. But we can pay it forward. And we do so each time we see someone's worth and potential so clearly that they come to see it in themselves.[17]

Executive presence. Seeing the next generation of leaders and helping them on their way has been a topic of conversation for Klaus and me since he was president of Microsoft in Europe and I led their one-year talent experience. In recent years, Klaus has chaired several boards and served on many more. I asked what he looks for when recruiting a new CEO. He wants leaders who are genuinely interested in people—because that is the source of followership and the reason AI can never lead. Klaus looks for those who want to know others as human beings, who see them.

How does he discern that in an interview? With this question: "Tell me about the people you have recruited and worked with who later in life reached positions that were equal to—or greater than—the one you have."

Few can answer it well, but for those who do, their stories tell him everything. They reveal their ability to spot future leaders, attract people of that caliber, and work alongside them. They coach and guide them. And then, when they no longer have the runway for that leader to grow, they help them on their way. Such candidates are leading with aliveness, and their network grows.

With the Power of Practice, we gain confidence; from confidence comes relaxation and flow, then timing and speed. The power is in the full-bodied presence of the referee, in the athlete in a state of flow, and in the incisive question of a chairperson.

WALKING TOWARD THE SWORD

"I don't know why you prepare so much," Wendy said. I dismissed her comment, for being well prepared is a virtue where I come from. Then, she'd bring it up again, and I'd explain how it allowed me to be more present during the session. She didn't buy it.

"What's your problem with me preparing so much?" I asked. Wendy looked me straight in the eye. "You can't grow into your potential." That got my attention. When I was younger, people would speak to my potential all the time, but it had been ages since anyone had done so.

We weren't done with the conversation, though. "You can't tell me that, with your experience, you couldn't show up unprepared and still lead a powerful session," Wendy said sometime later. Was that true? My head nodded, my heart said yes, and the core was a thumbs-up. It was unanimous. So why did I prepare so much?

The breakthrough came when I asked myself a slightly different question: *What's the difference between practice and excessive preparation?* Here's what I've learned. Practice expands our capacity to meet the moment as it is. Preparation anticipates problems and manages outcomes. Practice builds confidence; over-preparation reveals a lack of it.

Any irritation can become a prompt to practice. When stopping at a red light, slow down the exhale. When waiting in line, do a centering. When climbing the stairs, imagine a tailwind. If getting bored, run backward. Simply put: Notice the strain. Shift. Move with ease.

As we emerged from the pandemic, Wendy led her first retreat at my place in Spain. It would also be the last time we were to practice together—though she didn't know it, and neither did I. When she arrived, her ribs were sore, and we thought maybe she had pulled a muscle. Soon after, we learned it was cancer.

Even so, she gave us the gift of *walking toward the sword*—a way of training our capacity to face something fierce and deadly. It was a solemn ritual, done in silence, at the end of every retreat.

Wendy would walk to the center of the room with her *bokken* (a wooden sword) and assume the menacing posture of a warrior. Our task was to be present to our fear, center, and step forward.

One by one, we'd stand a few feet before her and bow. As she lifted the sword above her head, we'd walk straight toward her, and as she made the cut as if to split our skull, we'd find the space to pass, pivot, and pause right behind her. We would then circle each other, her fierceness palpable, and do it again.

In such moments, time slows down. We are attuned to the world around us. We are open a split second before something happens, anticipating rather than reacting, alert and at ease.

Wendy was my sensei for seven years.
And she saw me.
This chapter is dedicated to her.

What Power Do I Actually Have?

BJ FOGG, WHO HELPED DESIGN the dopamine loops behind LinkedIn and Instagram, is the founder of Stanford's Persuasive Technology Lab. In 2009, he renamed it the Behavior Design Lab—to focus on agency and wellness. In his words, "Emotions create habits. Not repetition. Not frequency. Not fairy dust. Emotions." Positive emotions immediately release dopamine, so we do the same thing again, and soon, we have a habit. This is the way to outsmart the algorithms and lead with aliveness.

We have the power to

~ Do a centering: use a prompt, center, and smile.

~ Clarify our intention before entering a meeting.

~ Close the door, and check with the head, heart, and core for inner coherence.

The challenge is this: We keep piling on. We push and plan and berate ourselves when we fall short. But the Power of Practice is not about discipline. Instead, all it takes is a predictable prompt, a tiny practice, and a touch of dopamine.

THE POWER OF THE
Pride

THE PRIDE OF THE SAVANNA

ALL FELINES HUNT ALONE—EXCEPT LIONS. Yet lions are the largest and most powerful of them all, so why hunt together? Because on the savanna, where time has shaped the balance between big herds and big cats, it was the prides that survived and thrived.

I encountered the Power of the Pride while working with a newly formed group of executives. The company had been growing at breakneck speed, sales were outrunning production, and margins were to die for. A private equity firm had acquired a majority stake, bought up the independent distributors from across the world, and was preparing to go public. Each leader was entrepreneurial and fiercely independent, having built their own operations and territories. Now the spreadsheet guys were moving in—and thus a clash of cultures. The new CEO had just a year to build the team at the top.

Four off-site sessions were designed, and the safari in South Africa became the seminal event. The jeeps rolled out at dawn and at dusk, a magical time in the bush, a time for thoughtful conversations. The giraffes looked at us curiously, and the leopards ignored us. And when a lion brushed by the open jeep, we barely breathed. We were in his territory.

The tracker Winnie Mathebula and the ranger Ian Thomas were a legendary team, known to have tracked and come to understand the dangerous lion Big Black, thus saving his life. Ian even dedicates his book to "Big Black, the most awesome lion I have ever encountered."

In *The Power of the Pride: How Lessons from a Pride of Lions Can Teach You to Create Powerful Business Teams*, Ian shares his love for the matriarchal hunting prides, in which trust is earned through competency. The big-shouldered lionesses lead the hunt, and the cubs learn from their mothers. They play at hunting: stalking, pouncing, wrestling, and testing their strength. They absorb the discipline by watching: the silent coordination, restraint, and explosive speed. They embody the lessons by doing.

Ian narrated a series of photos showing the big cats

drinking at a watering hole in the dark. In the first, a young lion lifted his ears. Was it an impala's alarm call? Instantly, all ears went up. They waited five seconds, then five more. When they heard the call again, the pride divided in two without a sound. Ten minutes later, they had dinner.

Some prides specialize in larger game, like water buffalo. The most experienced lioness makes the charge, and the others attack a split second later. The risks are immense, so why not settle for warthogs? Because they saw their elders do it and thought they could too. Because they believed, *We're the kind of pride that hunts water buffalo.*

Like the lions, we also have a shared identity—an inner knowing that we belong to a living system that requires our full participation. As the week went on, the conversation began to change, from "look at me and what I have built" to "look at us and what we might achieve together." What if they were to become the kind of pride that built a global brand and changed their industry?

As we said our goodbyes at the Londolozi Game Reserve, the team delivered a heartfelt message to the

CEO and CFO: Together, they could take care of the business and leave the CEO and CFO to do what only they could do: the high-stakes roadshow. Their combined efforts paid off, and five months later, the *Financial Times* reported on the largest IPO in Europe that year.

Our last session was in New York City. There, we completed the corporate values—pride, passion, and performance—each illustrated with a story. The pride signified competence and optimal performance. The giraffe, with its long neck and big heart, represented perspective and wholeheartedness. The bumblebee, a master of flexible flight, captured their entrepreneurial, can-do spirit.

We completed the journey by ringing the closing bell at Nasdaq. As we exited into Times Square, we saw the replay on the seven-story Nasdaq MarketSite: one pride, side by side, ringing the bell. Then, we had dinner.

AWAKENING THE PRIDE

The Power of the Pride is optimal performance, each member utterly capable and attuned to one another, each person fully who they are and fully part of the whole.[18]

To lead with aliveness, we must become a tracker of vitality, attuned to each person's energy, personality, and moves. To that end, what tracks might we look for?

In *Driven: How Human Nature Shapes Our Choices*, Paul Lawrence and Nitin Nohria draw on evolutionary biology and social sciences to identify four intrinsic sources of human motivation: acquire, bond, comprehend, and defend. I think of them as the A, B, C, and D of vitality.

Acquire fuels the pursuit of top grades, top schools, and top jobs—the drive to compete and win.

Bond fosters kindness, connection, and a sense of belonging—the drive to cooperate and win–win.

Comprehend sparks curiosity and the quest for meaning—the drive to explore and learn.

Defend guards one's resources and reputation— the drive to protect and defend.

All four drives are present in all of us, but to differing degrees—and in those variations lie our distinct forms of aliveness.

The strength of the pride is found in their collective commitment, the source of the *team effect*, according to Linda Hill and Kent Lineback, whose collaboration combines academic depth and executive experience. Their research shows that teams move as one when they know their work matters and when they believe the world is better off because of what they do. What holds such teams together is not their boss, but a web of mutual commitments and consequential goals.[19]

When the conditions are right, something powerful happens. Each person knows their role, reads the situation, anticipates problems, and adapts. They push, they play, they test each other's edges. They don't just do their jobs; they claim them. They become a dynamic force, a collective presence.

So what does the leader do? They give the team members the responsibility to grow and the space to move. They expand the Aliveness Effect.

PRIDE IN SPACE

When I met Thomas Marshburn, he had just returned from his third mission to the International Space Station (ISS), this time as the commander. Before becoming an astronaut, he had been an emergency room physician and a flight surgeon, and he clearly loved medicine. I wondered, *How did NASA take top performers and turn them into a coherent force?*

A mission in space involves a group of about a hundred people, with *ground* leading the mission and the *crew* in space. Every person in the astronaut corps is among the best in their field, be it operational, military, or scientific. So how do they get their egos out of the way? How do they come to move like a pride: in rhythm with themselves, with one another, and with the mission?

The key is to equalize the team. That begins with a swim test on day one, with everyone treading water for two minutes in full flight gear. This is tough for tiny people, and everyone gathers around to cheer them on. Operating excellence is easy for military commanders; team skills are a challenge for test pilots; and speaking Russian is hard for everyone. Part of being an astronaut is to be under constant scrutiny. There is rapid progression, and each team member is removed from their prior passion and area of excellence (for Tom, medicine). The toughest challenge of all is waiting for your assignment.

One day, when Tom and the other new astronauts were training in the pool, six of them were pulled into a high-fidelity simulation. They barely knew one another, yet they had to move as a pride. The minute they arrived, their commander (a veteran shuttle commander) told them they would start in about three minutes. "We don't know each other that well," he said. "I just want you to know that I'm going to screw up, and you are going to screw up, and I give you 0.2 seconds to get over it because I need you on this. So let's have at it."

Because of the commander's caliber and experience, revealing something like that was a superb setup, Tom told me. It reduced the astronauts' tension right away and raised their confidence.

At the end of Tom's second mission, ground reported an emergency: a coolant leak on the outside. The ISS was going to lose power, and without power, the situation would be disastrous. This is what they train for. Even so, it typically takes nine weeks to get ready for an extravehicular activity (EVA) like this. This time—from the moment ground had found the problem to the moment the astronauts were out the hatch—it was thirty-six hours.

Ground made the call because Tom and teammate Chris Cassidy knew each other really well, had done two EVAs together already, and had even been to the very site before. "Chris and I were thrilled we were going to do a space walk," Tom said with a grin. "We knew each other so well, we almost didn't have to talk to each other. And this time, we didn't worry we might mess up, for we had no procedures."

No training can prepare an astronaut for coming out of the hatch and looking straight down at Earth. It is disorienting, an assault on your entire physiological system. So they are taught to keep their world very small: "Release my hand." "Get my safety hook." "Click the handrail." "Take deep breaths." "Go slow." Within ten minutes, the physiological response evens out, and the training takes over. "Chris and I knew how to take care of ourselves and take care of each other, but we didn't know much more than that," Tom noted. "We literally went out the hatch and then waited for someone to call up the next step."

As in the sim, ground was in control, with the crew executing in space, and the repairs were made. This was a pride in action. No fanfare. No flex. Ultra.

IN THE ARENA

Lions are born into a pride, and as hunter-gatherers, so were we. I belong to the ocean and the land of my ancestors, who arrived at the top of the Danish peninsula during the Stone Age. The ocean was rough, the soil was sandy, and we were shaped by this place. We moved with the rhythms of the day, the seasons of the year, and the cycles of life.

Today, we may be part of several prides: call them teams, crews, or squads. And let's be clear: Being among the fans in the stands is not the same as being in the arena—a place of optimal performance, a place where you must be your best, not just professionally but fundamentally.

What earns us a place on the team? Our capacity

and competencies, our ability to handle pressure and respond skillfully. As leaders, what keeps us there is our capacity to grow—and to grow the next generation of leaders.

The strength of the pride lives in the depth of our connections—and healthy connections hold a positive charge that endures across time.

Leaders who connect create cultures of change, not because we talk culture, but because we are curious about people and their potential. We bring people together to get something done, and such connections speed up the interaction between two people or two groups and between the partners in an ecosystem.

There is strength in being connected. When our back is against the wall, we know someone to call (or know someone who knows someone), and that gives us confidence. We may not know what to do, but we know that together, we will find a way.

Being present to the life force in ourselves and seeing it in others is elemental—the source of leading with aliveness.

What Power Do I Actually Have?

IRENE WAS FIERCE, GENEROUS, and a wizard at turning around underperforming business units. She had no patience for the "What's in it for me?" mindset. In her words, "If you can't put the organization's interest ahead of your own comfort and change your behaviors, then you have no business being here." When doing a turnaround, she made the tough calls within six months. Her aim was a team that would work together and build those eyeball-to-eyeball, prick-your-finger-and-share-blood relationships. Here's how she answered the above question.

We have the power to

~ Envision an inspiring future and agree on what
  we believe in.

~ Know the right people, find the right people,
  and invite them to join.

~ Be humble, truly listen, and not think our ideas
  are the best.

~ Execute with absolute precision—and adapt.

The problem is that we are told to look out for ourselves, to build our own brand, to take responsibility
for our career. Yet to build a track record, we must
also build a real team. When leading with aliveness,
we do both.

THE POWER OF

Play

STEPPING INTO THE BOAT

AS HEAD OF THE AMERICAS for a multinational company, Rick was preparing for large-scale changes. The second time he came to New York for our work together, we walked across Midtown to the Hudson River. The moment he saw the water, Rick's energy shifted. This piqued my curiosity.

Here is what he told me: When Rick turned twelve, his father gave him an eighteen-foot sailboat, and thus began a series of adventures along the rivers of the Netherlands and the coastlines of Belgium and France. Then, he and his friends ventured across the English Channel, sailed up the Thames, and docked by Tower Bridge. By then, they knew that you must trust the crew you sail with: You have to sleep sometime— and each time you do, you put your life in their hands.

Upon graduating college, they decided to cross the

Atlantic, a journey that would take them from Rotterdam down to Faro, across to Las Palmas, and then the final stretch to St. Lucia. The rhythm was four hours on, four hours off. At the end of the nightshift, they'd make coffee, wake up others, and do the handover briefing. When they were not sailing, they fished and sorted the perishables for the least rotten food to eat.

After leaving Las Palmas, the ocean was rough. "We have twenty- to twenty-five-foot waves, and we're climbing up and surfing down those waves in a forty-seven-foot boat while it keeps rocking from side to side," Rick explained. "Up and down it goes. Up and down. Day after day, whether you are on deck, eating, or sleeping. It went on for seven days." With every step you take, you can really hurt yourself—not just by falling off the boat but by injuring yourself when you are on deck changing the sail. "You want to use both hands, but you *must* take care of yourself, for the boat needs all of us," Rick said. Thus, the sailor's caution: "one hand for yourself, the other for the boat."

There is no rational reason to make such a trip, so why do it? Because it is pure adventure, the Power of Play.

"Do you know what's worse than rough seas?" Rick then asked.

"No wind," I said.

He threw back his head and laughed. "Yes! We had two days when nothing moved and you go completely nuts."

Still, it did give them a chance to swim exactly in the middle of the Atlantic.

What left an indelible impression? On moonless nights, the deep dark of the sky seemed infinite and the stars so startlingly close; it was as if you were inside the universe. "Absorbing that, night after night, twenty-one nights in a row, is life changing," Rick added.

How did the adventure shape him as a leader? "It gave me a lot of confidence and made me realize that, when we want to, we can do serious things," he reflected. "We organized it ourselves, and we decided how much risk we were willing to take based on limited information. On the ocean, you live with the consequence. There is no stop model. No out."

EXPLORING PLAY

The Power of Play is pure adventure. Play is being so absorbed in an activity that it suspends our sense of time—on the edge of what we know, in contact with the unknown.

We are born as bundles of energy, inherently curious and ready to play, be it with our toes, sounds, or objects. As infants, we are like little scientists exploring the Aliveness Effect: forming hypotheses, testing, experimenting, and discovering.[20]

When faced with a puzzling problem, four-year-olds see the more creative solution more often than graduate students do, according to research by Alison Gopnik, who has studied children's ways of learning for decades. Why? Because as we grow up, the dynamic shifts from exploration to exploitation, from the joy of learning to getting good grades. We take Daniel Kahneman's[21] System 1, the source of intuitive connections and novel ideas, and put it under the management of System 2. We take joy and turn it into a job.

What would it look like to reclaim that balance? Consider my conversation with a London-based CEO, who was on the road most of the year. As we wrapped up a session with his executive team, I asked about his six-year-old daughter.

"I have two KPIs for her," he said.

I rolled my eyes, as if to say, "What am I going to do with you?"

He smiled. "That she sings when she gets up in the morning and when she goes to bed." A true performance indicator for aliveness.

Sometimes we sing alone and sometimes together. Sometimes we sing a ballad, sometimes the blues. And with our voices, we open the space for life to stream through.

At work, there is an inherent tension between the power of position and the Power of Play. To Peter Drucker, the twentieth-century sage on leadership, power was not a privilege; it was a responsibility. I agree. And I was inspired by Drucker's answer to a question about management theory, when he reportedly said, "I don't read management literature. I read Shakespeare."

So when the Royal Shakespeare Company visited the Brooklyn Academy of Music to perform the king series, I binge-watched *Richard II*, *Henry IV*, and *Henry V*. Each play was intense in its own right, and the cumulative effect was chilling. Recently, the Oscar-winning movie *Oppenheimer* had a similar effect.

The use and misuse of power is our history and our reality. But it is not our destiny. And given the magnitude of our problems, we must go beyond patterns of control to patterns of collaboration. Bill Sharpe, a guide on futures and living systems, shows there are three perspectives at play at all times. We all participate in all of them, and we can change them. His book *Three Horizons: The Patterning of Hope* shows how they work. Horizon 1 relies on the power of position: business as usual, keep the trains running, time is money. Horizon 3 opens to the Power of Play: emerging, pure adventure, time is destiny. Horizon 2 draws on both: testing ideas, placing bets, time is opportunity. Horizon 1 keeps us busy; Horizon 3 makes us bold.

Niels Bohr was a man of destiny. In *Oppenheimer*, we see him arriving at Los Alamos in 1943 and the deference shown to him. A junior physicist at the Manhattan Project at the time wrote that to them,

"Bohr was a living legend, the mind behind a new way of thinking about the universe, and a moral presence."[22]

But the legend didn't want to hear, "Yes, yes, Dr. Bohr." He wanted sparring partners and vigorous walks in the countryside. He wanted to *play*—to engage the entire extended mind.

OPPOSITES ARE COMPLEMENTARY

Educated in both physics and philosophy, Bohr believed that "the so-called 'deep truths,' are statements in which the opposite also contains deep truth."[23] He meant that in physics, philosophy, and life, apparent contradictions might hold essential parts of reality, depending on the scale or context. Thus, Bohr would famously say, "How wonderful that we have met with a paradox. Now we have some hope of making progress"[24]—meaning that they were nearing something fundamental.

In 1913, Bohr published his quantum model of the atom. In 1922, he received the Nobel Prize in Physics and opened the Institute for Theoretical Physics at the University of Copenhagen. The institute would become the intellectual epicenter for quantum mechanics in its formative years, often referred to simply as Copenhagen.

There, the most brilliant young minds of the century gathered together to bring order to the baffling aspects of behavior in the atomic world. There, the equations of the theory finally appeared, replacing the entire mechanics of Newton.[25] How was this possible? Because Bohr was alert to the power of his position and he relished the Power of Play.

In 1924, the young Werner Heisenberg arrived in Copenhagen, and his collaboration with Bohr became legendary, for they knew how to play. They walked for hours and argued late into the night. They wrestled with equations and the philosophical meaning of measurement, causality, and reality. They lost track of time and pushed each other's thinking to the breaking point. It was, according to Heisenberg, like attempting the high jump in a hurricane.

The outcome? In just three years, Heisenberg formulated matrix mechanics (1925) and the uncertainty principle (1927). And just eight years after arriving in Copenhagen, he was awarded the Nobel Prize in Physics for the creation of quantum mechanics.

Their work was so profound and unsettling that Einstein would grumble, "I, at any rate, am convinced that He (God) does not throw dice." To which Bohr famously replied, "Einstein, stop telling God what to do."

LIFE IS IN THE TENSION

How did Bohr navigate the uncertainty of the burgeoning science, the skeptics, the harsh realities of the war, and its aftermath?[26] With a deep inner knowing, an embodied sense of wisdom, a philosophy, if you will.

Before receiving the Order of the Elephant (the Danish knighthood) in 1947, Bohr was asked to create a personal coat of arms. His shield bears the traditional symbol of the yin-yang, rendered in black and ruby red, and his motto *Contraria Sunt Complementa* (opposites are complementary). This was the tension in which he played, a space of profound insights, present to the primordial power.

This past spring, while sorting some papers, I found a yellowed piece of newspaper with an op-ed by a philosopher. Heavily underlined were these words: "The goal of life, for Pascal, is not happiness, peace, or ful-fillment but aliveness."[27] I was barely familiar with Blaise Pascal, but I resonated with the sentiment. Now I knew why.

Here is how I see it: Happiness rests in content-ment; aliveness brings us awake. Peace seeks resolution; aliveness needs tension. Fulfillment marks completion; aliveness begins again.

The anthropologist Albert Kroeber put it this way: "The ideal situation for any individual or any culture is not bovine placidity. It is rather the highest state of ten-sion that the organism can creatively bear"—because cultures and people flourish not by eliminating tension but by mastering it.[28]

PURE ADVENTURE

Each summer, I move from the canyons of New York City to the coastal cliffs of Galicia, Spain. There, my chest fills with the salted air, the trees are shaped by the wind, and the sun sets in the ocean. Just like home.

At dawn, I walk to the bluffs with my *bokken* to begin the cuts—precise, practiced arcs—and say my "prayers" to the sea, my intention for the day: a short sentence and a strike, repeated again and again, orienting my body and mind to the same intention.

One morning, as I stepped onto the outcropping, the sky turned dark, and the wind blew up. The swells surged, and the spray reached above the cliffs. The heavens opened; water from above and below blurred into one. As I raised the *bokken* above my head, the wind almost ripped it from my hands. As I made the cut, I laughed out loud: "I open to the Power of Play in a big way today."

What if instead of resisting uncertainty, we were to relish it—to go beyond anxiety to awe? What if we were to look up at the stars on a moonless night and feel we were inside the universe, ready for high jumps in hurricanes—open to the Power of Play?

What Power Do I Actually Have?

I LOVE THE BIG APPLE—the tempo, the talent, the restless ambitions. I relish walking across the Brooklyn Bridge to the Fulton Ferry Landing, where stamped into the railing are the words of Walt Whitman: the poet who gave voice to the energy of the streets and the democratic ideals of the city. As I walk the railing, I read his words aloud: "Throb, baffled and curious brain! throw out questions and answers!"

We have the power to

- ~ Get excited by paradox, as it signals something fundamental.
- ~ Be more expansive—to sing when we get up and when we go to bed.
- ~ Test promising leaders by treating them as true sparring partners.

We are bringing immense, possibly ungovernable, technologies into every part of our lives. And we must match the scale of our creations with the depth of our conscience. Pause sooner. See what's at stake. Take a stand.

Go Beyond

LEADING WITH ALIVENESS

SO HERE WE ARE. WE'VE been to the mountains, walked across campus, and stood on top of the world. We've gone on safari, sailed the Atlantic, and stayed in Copenhagen. Each story an inspiration for leading with aliveness.

Where do we go from here?

Given the uncertainty, how do we prepare when we don't even know what to look for—let alone where to find it? And if we find it, we can't know how fast it's moving. Because as soon as we focus on one thing, the other slips away.

Again, we return to the question, *What power do I actually have?*

When we open to the Power of the Pause, we go beyond stress to strength; with the Power of Perspective, beyond busy to bold; and with the Power of

Practice, beyond words to voice. We open to all that life offers—the bitter, the beautiful, the brave.

With the Power of the Pride, we push each other, and we pick each other up when we fall down—no longer doubtful but decisive. And with the Power of Play, we go beyond anxiety to awe. We marvel at the Aliveness Effect.

We live in a time of cascading crises—climate, conflict, collapse. Yet even with the churn of disruption, something elemental remains: the universal energy, the life force, the source of aliveness.

When we open to the deepest powers of leadership, we feel the pulse, we sense the hidden wholeness and wonder what role we may play.

That is leading with aliveness.

Acknowledgments

TO THE LEADERS IN THE ARENA, to the ones who show up every day. To those who lead with aliveness—who shared their stories. And to the clients and colleagues whose feedback guided this work.

To Tina Chang, CEO of Pioneering Collective, who built an executive network founded on generosity—a spirit that infused our collaboration from the beginning.

And to Ernie Sander, whose rapid-fire questions made me see there was still a book to write.

To Rick Rubin, whose reflections on the creative act carried the early stages.

And to George Saunders, for whom revising is like holding a tuning fork to a sentence—listening for the energy.

To Liya James, whose brush and attention brought the early chapters to life.

And to Sheila Parr, whose cover design radiates aliveness.

To Scott James, who, at every fork, pointed to the path least traveled. As my writing coach and companion, he saw what was alive in me—and in the work.

To Alfredo Gomez—my husband, my love—who sees me, and who has been by my side through every business and creative adventure.

And now, the work begins to speak for itself.

Notes

1. Dan Hoyer et al, "All Crises Are Unhappy in Their Own Way: The Role of Societal Instability in Shaping the Past," *SocArXiv Papers*, February 15, 2024. This article describes 168 crises characterized by significant "consequences" such as civil war, epidemics, or loss of population.

2. Giuseppe Verdi, *La forza del destino* revised libretto, 1869. In the early performances, all the main characters died, and that turned out to be too bleak, even for opera lovers. After a rewrite, a monk survives.

3. UrbanPromise was founded by Bruce Main and Pamela Burgess Main in 1988, in Camden, New Jersey. Jim Cummings joined UrbanPromise in 2004, when he launched UrbanTrekkers. All three are now in the leadership of UrbanPromise International.

4. John Coates, "The Uncertainty Principle," *Financial Times*, May 10, 2025.

5. Carlo Rovelli, *Seven Brief Lessons on Physics*, trans. Simon Carnell and Erica Segre (New York: Riverhead Books, 2016).

6. After the Covey Leadership Center merged with Franklin Quest, it became FranklinCovey.

7. A program hosted by the Center for Higher Ambition Leadership, now the Higher Ambition Leadership Alliance.

8. Douglas Conant and Mette Norgaard, *TouchPoints: Creating Powerful Leadership Connections in the Smallest of Moments* (San Francisco: Jossey-Bass, 2011).

9. Birgit Signora Toft, *Pausens kraft: Sådan tanker du op* (Copenhagen: Gyldendal Business, 2010).

10. Seamus Heaney, "Postscript," in *The Spirit Level* (London and New York: Faber and Faber, 1996): "A hurry through which known and strange things pass / As big soft buffetings come at the car sideways / And catch the heart off guard and blow it open."

11. With smart rings, bracelets, and watches, we become aware of the body's natural rhythms—shaped by our chronotype. With biofeedback and resonance breathing, we can enter flow in a few breaths. And with neurofeedback, we can slow down our high-beta brain waves. We can work with our body's capacity to push and restore itself; that is physiological intelligence.

12. Gloria Mark, *Attention Span: A Groundbreaking Way to Restore Balance, Happiness and Productivity* (New York: HarperCollins, 2023). Mark cites research showing that the average attention on any given screen has

declined from about 2½ minutes in 2004 to less than 47 seconds today.

13. Stephen J. Dubner, host, *Freakonomics Radio, episode* 306, "How to Launch a Behavior-Change Revolution." Freakonomics Radio Network.

14. Ed Catmull, "The Key to Pixar's Creativity," interview at *Fortune Brainstorm Tech Conference*, Aspen, CO, July 2019.

15. Bill Bryson, *The Body: A Guide for Occupants* (New York: Vintage Books, 2021).

16. Peter M. Senge et al., *The Fifth Discipline Fieldbook: Strategies and Tools for Building a Learning Organization* (New York: Doubleday, 1994).

17. Stephen R. Covey, *The 8th Habit: From Effectiveness to Greatness* (New York: Free Press, 2004).

18. Bill Sharpe, *Three Horizons: The Patterning of Hope* (Axminster: Triarchy Press, 2013). Bill inspired the sentiment that we can be fully who we are and fully part of the whole.

19. Linda A. Hill and Kent Lineback, *Being the Boss: The 3 Imperatives for Becoming a Great Leader* (Boston: Harvard Business Review Press, 2011). Linda A. Hill et al., *Collective Genius: The Art and Practice of Leading Innovation* (Boston: Harvard Business Review Press, 2014).

20. Alison Gopnik, Andrew N. Meltzoff, and Patricia K. Kuhl, *The Scientist in the Crib: What Early Learning Tells Us About the Mind* (New York: William Morrow, 1999).

21. Daniel Kahneman, *Thinking, Fast and Slow* (New York: Farrar, Straus and Giroux, 2011).

22. Richard P. Feynman, *"Surely You're Joking, Mr. Feynman!": Adventures of a Curious Character*, ed. Ralph Leighton (New York: W. W. Norton, 1985).

23. Niels Bohr: refers to this as a familiar adage in "Discussion with Einstein on Epistemological Problems in Atomic Physics", printed in *Albert Einstein: Philosopher–Scientist* (edited by P. A. Schilpp).

24. *Niels Bohr: The Man, His Science, & the World They Changed* (1966) by Ruth Moore

25. Carlo Rovelli, *Seven Brief Lessons on Physics*, trans. Simon Carnell and Erica Segre (New York: Riverhead Books, 2016).

26. Most of the leading theoretical physicists, many of them Jewish, fled Europe in the 1930s while Heisenberg continued his work under the Nazi regime. As the war deepened, each grappled with the burden of conscience. Michael Frayn captures their struggles in *Copenhagen*, his Tony Award-winning play about Heisenberg's clandestine visit to Bohr in 1941 (London: Methuen Drama, 1998). After the war, Bohr sent an open letter to the United Nations, one of the clearest early calls to match scientific power with global responsibility (*Open Letter to the United Nations*. Copenhagen: J. H. Schultz Forlag, June 9, 1950).

27. Sean D. Kelly, "Waking Up to the Gift of 'Aliveness,'" *New York Times*, December 25, 2017.

28. Thomas Berry, *The Dream of the Earth* (San Francisco: Sierra Club Books, 1988).